THE ANSWER TO LORD CHANDOS

THE ANSWER TO LORD CHANDOS

Pascal Quignard

INTRODUCTION BY JEAN-LUC NANCY

translated by Stéphanie Boulard

and Timothy Lavenz

■

WAKEFIELD PRESS

CAMBRIDGE, MASSACHUSETTS

Wakefield Press, P.O. Box 425645, Cambridge, MA 02142

Originally published as *La Réponse à Lord Chandos* in 2020.
© Pascal Quignard, 2020

This work received support for excellence in publication and translation from Albertine Translation, formerly French Voices, a program of Albertine Foundation in partnership with Villa Albertine.

This book was set in Garamond Premier Pro and Helvetica Neue Pro by Wakefield Press. Printed and bound by Versa Press in the United States of America.

ISBN: 978-1-939663-93-1

Available through D.A.P./Distributed Art Publishers
75 Broad Street, Suite 630
New York, New York 10004
Tel: (212) 627-1999
Fax: (212) 627-9484

10   9   8   7   6   5   4   3   2   1

CONTENTS

LITERATURE VERSUS LITERATURE

1

Hofmannsthal's *Letter from Lord Chandos to Lord Bacon*, published in 1902, lays claim to a remarkable privilege: the few pages of this text have given rise to hundreds, if not thousands, of commentaries and interpretations. A number of these have taken the form of a response, since the *Letter* presents itself as a response to another letter. It is perhaps the Germans who have played this game the most, for in their language "answer"—*Antwort*—literally signifies "word (*Wort*) in return," and, as we know, "the word" or "words" are the object of the *Letter*, these "words of language" which "seem to drive into the abyss" the writer. The Latin–French *réponse* does not evoke words: however, it does take on a *responsibility*, namely to do justice to that which one responds to, ensuring it is well considered and, if necessary, irreversibly refuted.

That indeed is the side Quignard is on. Right from the start, his Bacon declares to Hofmannsthal's Chandos that he "does not agree" to his letter and even "disapproves" of it. In fact, his answer—much more developed than the *Letter*—leads a vehement and uncompromising charge against the disqualification of the words of language that drove Chandos to decide to stop writing (at least nothing literary, nothing we would call "writing") and to instead entrust himself to the "mute and often inanimate" presence of the humblest creatures. Everything became "something" for him, and the exact nature of this "something," its presence and its mystery, is not a matter for language.

Quignard–Bacon retorts that without language we would not even have access to this "first world." At the bottom of things, there is not silence but rather what he names, after the example of waves, a "*tidal bore of life.*" As he writes at the end, one is dazzled only after having seen.

2

The *disputatio* summed up in this way suffers no negotiation, no dialectical sublation. Precisely where Hofmannsthal, along with an entire era, had his doubts about language, Quignard—going rather against his time—affirms its necessity and its power. He does not argue that words open onto things, but rather that they lead "letter by letter" to the possibility of feeling out "*more and more the night, the origin, the abyss.*"

This does not prevent him from recognizing the loftiness and beauty of the letter from Chandos. Likewise, if Hofmannsthal could read Quignard's letter, he certainly would not fail to praise its literary quality. And so one is led to believe that we are witnessing, with this exchange that spans more than a century, a great scene internal to literature, a scene condensed here into a startling distillation. Literature began to distrust itself at the dawn of the twentieth century, beginning with Nietzsche and Mauthner (much read by Hofmannsthal). At the beginning of the twenty-first century, we doubt instead if literature still takes place. Hofmannsthal's recoil before words responds to the wear and tear of a certain grandiloquence and literary profusion of the nineteenth century. The vibrant defense of those same words, in Quignard, responds to a banalization and informatization of language ushered in by the twentieth century.

And yet, distrust of literature may well be as old as literature itself. In effect, it appears when philosophy strips myth and tragedy of their legitimacy. Philosophy wants to take care of the concept, which ultimately must be subtracted from words, and so it casts suspicion on any trust in the latter. "To know things in themselves" is the formula Socrates opposes to Cratylus, who wanted the names of things to have been instituted by some divinity in accordance with their nature. If Lord Chandos writes to Francis Bacon (whom Hofmannsthal also read), it is because of the nominalism that launched modernity by dissipating the reality of metaphysical authorities—which no doubt contributed to the literary flowering of his time, since the less that concepts touch the real, the more precious becomes the imaged, conjured, sung reality. But also the decorative, precious, even artificial forms spread out more. Over the centuries, one will become suspicious of rhetoric, preciousness, "beautiful style," the novel and poetry … It is not by chance that in 1882 Verlaine concludes his *Ars Poetica* thus:

> May your verse be a fortunate adventure
> Scattered in the brisk morning wind
> Which wanders smelling of thyme and mint …
> And all the rest is literature.

The dispute we are witnessing here is consubstantial with literature, for it avoids sacred language as much as the conceptual subsumption of language.

3

It is also for this reason that a very careful reading of these texts, the *Letter* and the *Answer*, is necessary. First, one must consider their respective titles. Hofmannsthal's is strictly speaking *A Letter*, and it is only under this title that the Lord Chandos text is introduced—by the words "Here is the letter ..." Who undertakes this introduction? That is not stated: neither a narrator nor an archivist, no one is designated. It is indeed a matter of the literary author, of this author who is present by his absence and who is never the prophet of a god, nor an anonymous supplier of documents. The author is here, as everywhere in literature, the literary capacity or the literary disposition itself, which addresses, even addresses to itself, a missive on its own subject. It enters into a dialogue about itself with itself, and this dialogue focuses on its own relationship to the real because it assumes by its very nature that it is neither the expression nor the truth of the real. For Lord Chandos, in sum, it must go beyond itself and cede its place to an immediate presence, the only irrefutable presence of this real.

Quignard's title, on the other hand, announces itself as *The Answer to Lord Chandos*: directly addressed to the fictional subject of the letter, it plays its game and situates itself inside the fiction, but it does so as "the" determined and unambiguous response that would arrive within this very interior to denounce the denunciation of literature. Literature must instead be affirmed as the diction of the real itself in its unassignable profundity. It is in literature that the reality of the real happens.

Through this manifest opposition, Hofmannsthal and Quignard are closer than it may appear. The first actually seeks not mutism so much as an *other* language. Near the end of his letter, he evokes its deepest motive: "a language in which mute things sometimes speak to me and in which perhaps, once in the grave, I will be able to answer for myself before an unknown judge." "Answer" here means *verant-worten*—where, as in French, the response takes on responsibility.

Quignard plays the role of just such a judge, and he cannot help but hear the answer he anticipates from the one he wants to answer. For while he vigorously orders him not to "confuse the silences," he will still have to admit that, without being very explicit about it, Hofmannsthal did not exactly confuse them. From his "silence" to Quignard's, there is indeed a certain continuity. From one to the other, of course, is the distance of a century that separates a discontent before words too broad and vague (in romanticism as well as in symbolism) and a sense of the inaccessible "night, origin, abyss" that emerged from Freud, from Heidegger, and finally from the many collapses of the Western world. It would be very strange if the second silence were simply in agreement with the first. But it should not be overlooked that the first paved the way for the second. If, thanks to words, the latter wants to "feel out the night," the former writes that "those insignificant creatures, a dog, a rat, […] a stone were more to me than the most beautiful, most abandoned of lovers on the happiest of nights."

It is not the same night, but it is always a matter of penetrating, experiencing, and traversing the night, be it always into more night. For the one as for the other, it is a passionate transport into the "whirlwinds" or into an "ecstasy," which are always figures of literature as an approach, neither sacred nor conceptual, to the bottomless depth of the world.

Now we have the letter and its answer, both of them incomparable and yet inclined toward one another and by one another.

Jean-Luc Nancy, April 2021

THE ANSWER TO
LORD CHANDOS

1

EMILY IN THE SHADOW
OF THE ST. GUDULA BELL TOWER

———————

In 1842, on Rue Isabelle, in Brussels, when she was teaching at the Heger boarding school, Emily Brontë never raised her eyes toward the other professors. She went only once into the room reserved for them; the panic attack that seized her then was such that she never set foot in it again. If someone watched her closely while she was eating at the refectory table, she would look away, confused, filled with a dizzying fear, although she was never fearful of anything in England, in the Yorkshire, when she was out on her own and roamed the moor in the company of her dog and her goshawk, when she encountered vagabonds and crossed paths with madmen there. She never had the courage to address her colleagues when she bumped into them in the hallways and they took her to task in a discussion; she rapidly bowed her head. Even the students to whom she taught English literature and music, she did not look at. She spoke a very beautiful and ceremonious French. She kept her hands buried in the thick fabric of her dresses. In the evening, she trembled, a stranger among strangers, cornered between the curtain screen at her bed and the tiny windowpanes that hung over the armoire and the nightstand. She buried her face deep in the faintly prickly feathers of her pillow, and there she wept for a long time in silence. In the morning, with the copper bars slicing into her back, hidden behind the curtain, protected by its screen, in the first ray of sunlight, leaned up against her pillow, she read in the shadows cast by the St. Gudula bell tower. When her sister asked how things were going for her, if this life was bearable despite everything, she limited her response to: "I am glad to have a curtain at my bed."

✳

Emily Brontë played Rameau on the harpsicord.

Sometimes she arranged old songs by Handel, thinning them out and adding a bit of white gouache to make them at once easier to interpret, more convenient to memorize, and more touching to recognize.

Before deciding to play any of the scores, seated at Mr. Heger's living room table, she would hear it in her head. Her hands, without anyone seeing them move, would play on an imaginary keyboard. Then she would write, on the score, the fingerings above *all* the notes.

At the Heger boarding school, she did not even dare show the students in her care, at the end of the hour, the piece she had asked them to learn for the next lesson.

She started to hide her hands inside the sleeves of her waistcoat, or to slide them under the points or flaps of her bodice. She did not like her hands because, no longer going outside, no longer kneading bread, no longer planting or pulling up vegetables in the garden, they had become entirely white, soft, refined, her fingernails round and clean, feminine, delightful.

Emily Brontë declared to her sister, her father, two vicars, two maidservants, when she returned to the vicarage at Haworth:

"Starting today I demand that no one interfere with my desire to stay away. Away from visitors, of course. Away from suppliers, that goes without saying. But also away from the other family members, all the cousins, nieces, aunts. From now on I want to be left alone. To look after the poor, to bring tea to visiting pastors, that is beyond my strength."

(Freedom, according to Emily Brontë's conception of it, is not a state. It is an irrepressible drive for emancipation that carries us away the moment we leave the maternal womb, and in her eyes it is infinite. Freedom is the preservation of that original personal isolation. It stems from fetal self-entanglement, so similar to the movement made by fern buds in their tiny croziers before they unfold. This unity, which is also a union with self, exists prior to the dual relation (which is established as soon as the mother feeds her suckling infant by tendering her breast and inclining her gaze), prior to the ternary relation that inaugurates grammar (to which the name of King Oedipus has been nobly associated), prior to plural and familial relations (submissive and puerile), school relations (adolescent and shame-inducing), and collective relations (the rights and duties of citizens). This way of understanding the destiny of days and the evolution of ages is close to the teachings of Buddhism: liberation from the successive stages of morphogenesis, then of phylogenesis, then from the hierarchy of social classes, then from the benefits and agonizing restraints of civilization. One morning, as night was coming to a close, Prince Shakyamuni rose from his bed without making a sound, left his wife forever, stepped over the body of his sleeping son, went out from his father's palace, reached a tree at the water's edge and leaned up against its trunk: until his death he stayed there, seated in the shadow of its branches.)

✻

PASCAL QUIGNARD

Mrs. Margot Peters reports this secret Charlotte Brontë confided to her about her sister Emily:

"My sister Emily watched over her private life like a miser over his gold. She said she hated society, but actually I think it would be fairer to say she didn't care. She loved nature, the moorland, clouds, birds, running. She adored her dog Keeper. She named her bird of prey Fusely after the painter Füssli, who spent his life dreaming."

2

GEORGE HANDEL IN HANOVER SQUARE

————————

Sir John Hawkins said of George Handel: "Mr. Handel never needed society."

Aside from his long stays with Lord Chandos and Lord Shaftesbury when it came time to write operas, since then he had to concentrate fully, panoramically, painfully on the composition of those grand ensembles, Handel never left London. (Shaftesbury and Chandos reserved for him, in every castle they owned, a small apartment perfectly sealed off, so he would feel at home in it. When he was there, no one was allowed to enter except for servants to change the linens, do the cleaning, make the bed, fill the fireplace with wood. And that was only when they saw him walking in the park and heading to the forest. Or when he was dining in the great hall.)

He had no desire to see Germany again.

In London, he hardly ever left the house he had acquired near Hanover Square.

Three windows twice on the facade.

Two stories above a basement floor taking light from the pavement of the street with the help of a long solid wood shutter that lifted like a guillotine; it housed the long kitchen where the cook and a servant lived and slept.

The handyman, who acted mostly as a gardener, lodged in one of the garden huts.

There were two rooms on each level. The larger one opened onto the street. The smaller one onto the courtyard, where the lilac tree, the climbing rosebush, the green vine, the walnut tree, and the well stood out.

Finally, if you lingered a while, you could see the wheelbarrow.

The rake for the dead leaves.

The watering can placed under the rain gutter that came down from the roof.

He always said *eine Geisskanne* for the iron watering can, *ein Nussbaum* for the walnut tree.

Inside Handel's small living room—according to the inventory made after his death—there was a large secretary made of walnut, a water bowl, a full-length mirror ringed with brass, and two striking wooden heads on which his wigs were placed. Two big heads without eyes or mouth, so that the wigs, reeking with sweat and smoke, could dry out when the evenings were over. So that the smell of society and its solicitations, its judgments, its resentments, its heartbreaks, were not brought any further into the house.

In the large living room that opened onto the street, a deep fireplace ringed with red-veined marble, some thick red velvet curtains (which reached to the floor and shielded the room from the noise of carriage wheels or horseshoes), one large Ruckers organ, one newer André that had been tuned by Lambert Hatten, one small positive organ.

A bookcase with scores stacked one on top of the other.

An oval table in Württemberg marquetry.

A porcelain tea service from Saxony.

On the wall just one large Rembrandt. It is the extraordinary *View of the Rhine*. That is all. Handel's only luxury.

It is perhaps the most beautiful work (along with *The Three Trees* etching) by the great Dutch painter who lived above that little harbor, in the marvelous second-floor workshop on Sint Anthonisdijk and the canal, in Breestraat, a stone's throw from the ghetto.

In many ways, that somber river, when he sets his eyes on it, reconnects the composer to his childhood, to his mother's birthplace, to violent weather, to the incredible beauty of nature, to the origin.

✳

I have often accompanied the *Neun Deutsche Arien* on baroque cello. Whenever an opera singer from the baroque world or even from the romantic world wished to sing them, we made every effort to follow her voice, the force, the vibrato or detaché of her breath, the ornaments of her plaint. For grief has something luxurious about it, something of a great river, in the same way that tears present something that diverts us from grief's grip by its flow, by its sobbing, and even dissipates it. Yannick Guillou owned, in Paris, on Rue Solférino, three fabulous harpsichords. I used to come by foot with my cello over my shoulder. I lived on Quai des Grands-Augustins then, facing Notre-Dame. All I had to do was walk along the Seine, the strap of the case that held the cello pressing against my shoulder. Gérard Dubuisson, meanwhile, came from Rue de l'Odéon with a wooden box for his violin. He walked down Boulevard Saint-Germain. Either he played the violin part or he sang. Most often Yannick chose the Ruckers, and I sat down by his side. I picked a tapestried pouffe, entrusting the base of the cello and all the movements I put it through to my calves. I balanced like a pendulum, I drove in my nails, I danced beside the harpsichord stool. The *Neun Deutsche Arien* is Handel's deeply moving farewell to his mother. There was a recording we made of it once, if I remember correctly, with Mrs. Klett Cotta. Playing with the spouse of this publisher whose name is so old and so prestigious, one felt a bit like Hölderlin was near. I so love these short circuits of places and times—the way cats delight in skylights, in cracks, in crossbars on the rooves, between the chimneys and the gutters. We drank a red Burgundy wine into which Gérard Dubuisson mixed some blackcurrant liqueur from Dijon to blacken it even more. As for Handel, it was Lord Radnor who supplied him with Burgundy wine, which had made the jump across the English Channel through Dieppe, at the bottom of big sea barges.

In Hanover Square, on the second floor, past the antechamber where he laid down his clothes, where the close stool stood, was Handel's master bedroom: a large blue and white earthenware stove from Basel, a bed with curtains, two bolsters, two pillows, several covers, a blue satin eiderdown.

He worked in bed.

On the bedside table, the stemmed glass and the bottle of Burgundy that was uncorked each night before going to sleep, to get to sleep.

✳

To verify what he had composed during the night, to improvise as well, simply to dream and make his way in his sonorous dream, Handel employed the great Ruckers of 1612 in the downstairs room systematically. The instrument dates back to the Chandos who was Lord Bacon's friend. The younger Lord Chandos wrote: "The boxwood keys were worn down, hollowed out, as if before one's eyes were a service of small vermeil spoons."

Around the old harpsichord, seven chairs for the musicians, the choirmasters, the singers, the lords.

Two small round walnut tables so that any of them could, on occasion, take down their notes or do their calculations, draw their quick sketches.

In the wide porphyry fireplace, the andirons were adorned with terrifying wolves' heads with gaping mouths.

✳

Hugo von Hofmannsthal suffered a terrible nervous breakdown that began the month of November 1899,

PASCAL QUIGNARD

right at the turn of the century, though his despair did not have to do with this turn.

His distress had to do with love and marriage.

This pain lasted a year and a half.

He published, in 1902, his *Lord Chandos*—which became my Handel.

In 1978, after a new depression had come and also made itself at home in those long nights only winter can devise, I started drafting a response to the letter from 1603.

In Hofmannsthal's prodigious account, written in 1901, Lord Chandos's letter is dated 22 August 1603 (A.D. 1603 diesen 22 August) when he was in Rome. I invented a letter dated 23 April 1605, which I then attributed to Francis Bacon Lord Verulam, in response to the letter from Lord Chandos of 1901–1603.

3

BACON TO CHANDOS

———————

Francis Lord Verulam, viscount of Saint Alban, to Philipp Lord Chandos, 23 April 1605, I have let the seasons drag on. I have left unanswered the letter you addressed to me two years ago, which you wrote at the end of the summer. Even if the time to apologize is long past, I nevertheless ask for your pardon. Age, worries, duties, pleasures too, even the accumulation of wealth, laziness still more, please understand, I shall say no more, it all means nothing, but it all does gnaw the hours. Even, sometimes, life seems bitten by it. Or it is continually and *deliberately* wounded by it. And besides, how could I hide it from you? It was all a pretext to keep me from writing you, for I did not agree to your letter. The very loftiness of your letter's ponderings, your sadness, its beauty, my dissent, everything came to be an obstacle. And the delay increased, and the time I let slip away kept slipping away, everything became an escape to avoid showing my disapproval, to not quibble with you, to not lack compassion or sensitivity with you in your despondency, I kept running away—but it is enough to name the importunities, the duties, the lassitudes, the setbacks, the time. The simple word time. For it is always empty time that passes and nothing else inside it. Just as in our bodies this blood flows and pounds. And always it rushes to its own immeasurable beat. And it takes a hundred cables to hail this incredible pulse, to divert this flow to a task, guide it to a letter, open the writing desk, uncap the inkwell, grab the bird's feather—when any little wave knocks it down. Even a tear knocks it down. But let us forget about time, life, the pulse, death, distraction, the arts, music, tears, and get to the bottom of it. For this bottom concerns something that is even more serious in my eyes than your despair was, and that is silence. *Your* silence. Your silence faced with the whole of language, against which you oppose it. For this is not *my* silence. Hence I take leave of time and apply myself directly to *your* silence. I cannot deny it: I am in head-on disagreement with the letter you wrote back then. What sticks with me are all your digressions; they are marvelous— though they are only so marvelous, truth be told, because they are marvelously said. But it is an illusion as to the substance. Your reflection builds on sand. It raises a dam that is merely sublime, secondary, sentimental. Beware: I think that in *beauty* itself there is something cowardly that hides, that doesn't want to aggress, that retreats

PASCAL QUIGNARD

from the real, and maybe that alone was enough to corrupt your thought. You *renounce* poetry. How wrong you are! You are a great poet. Your conception of silence comes directly from Epicurus. This "illusion of silence" upstream of the acquisition of language, and even the idea of "language at rest" with regard to an artifice that is, however, nothing like an animal that can experience fatigue, are by no means convincing or strong. Even, I thought when reading you that your thought had something impossible about it. And, even worse than impossible, something fundamentally ungrateful. Who could be quit of language—truly quit of it, perfectly weaned—when he has so painstakingly and for so long and *willingly* made it his own during the seven years that count for childhood, before the latent years that conclude it or rather ratify it? This is perhaps the reason why your letter was so long, interminable, and why it requires in return a response that will itself be, in all likelihood, interminable. It certainly constituted, in your eyes, in the depths of your soul, a painful confession. You denounced an ordeal caused by the condition of human speech that can only remain in the state of speech. That is true. But never, do you hear, never will you escape the language in whose sound your mother cradled you to the point that she was able to immerge you in it permanently. Never. Even in the other world your soul will not be free of it. If there is an imprint, it is received from language. No one can be *liberated* from this invasion when one *took off the lock* oneself in times past. Always, in the human being who has learned a language, the old world that rushes inside his need, his hunger, his desire, and the new world of grammar, rhetoric, tradition, and religion, clash without ever marrying. The tortoise and Achilles race eternally—even if one can observe an eternal advantage for the originary. Achilles is just a name, he is no more than a mythical hero who speaks in verse of six feet, while the tortoise is an animal who swims in the sea and tucks in his head to push it forward continuously by opening his jaws to a shred of real flesh. The inexpressible is nothing real. The inexpressible is a *contrast of language* that comes after its agreed-upon, servile, laborious apprenticeship. But the upstream of language is not silence. Listen to the birds in the dawn. Listen to the infants before they learn to speak! Go down to the beach at the foot of your father's castle, where the bay that goes to the port begins. Listen to the sea before life! For we who are blessed to live on an island, this noise is more powerful and frightening than every human language combined. Now compare this to the little story made up by the life of one man. Odysseus had grown old. Odysseus had fought for years with the sea, against the sea, facing the inexpiable, irremissible hostility of the god of the sea. Odysseus had known pleasure, royalty, the hunt, war, glory, shipwreck, poverty, the shaggy filth, the shame of nudity on the edge of the beach of the island of the Phaeacians, the constant nearness of death to which he kept coming ever closer, recklessly, almost avidly. Yes, Odysseus falls silent then, but it is over the *story* of his life that he pulls the tablecloth and wraps his nose, his mouth, his eyes, his ears in it. The silence wherein he shuts himself away is only a hiding place. The whole legend the bard sings is not his life. He covers his face because he is seized with shame! He hides his features because he weeps! Or perhaps Odysseus, in this unexpected silence, delights not in the *memory* of his life in his sensation, but in the *return* of his life in the language the bard sings so incomparably before him, with the help of his lyre, by showing off, by plucking the strings with his plectrum, by inventing episodes, by historiating them, by embellishing them, by cutting them up, by letting the sound that punctuates them ring out before the banqueters, before the young princess, before King Alcinous. He enjoys them then because he discovers his adventures suddenly projected outside the enigma of having to live them. For a life is not a story. You yourself, Philipp Lord Chandos, were twenty-six years old when you wrote me your anguished letter. Now you are twenty-eight. You are still so young! You still touch infancy! But the silence you imagined then was not the silence that stood at the heart of your infancy yet so near. That silence is constructed the way language is acquired. That *rhetorical* silence may, certainly, provide its support *after the fact*, serving as cover, screen, tablecloth, as taciturn reticence, modesty, secrecy; but the rhetoric that penetrates to the heart of things transforms them all without exception, and this metamorphosis is as irremediable as the virulent and limitless hatred with which Poseidon surrounds Odysseus over the course of different shipwrecks that make up his wandering. The common exercise of language divides. Its true face is the dialogue. Silence, thus placed in a second position, is only an impossible *flight* out of the mediation it imposes. A wing that fades into the sky and is no longer perceived there, not even in the dispersion of winds, no matter how hard the eyes attempt to find its aspect, which cannot even become a memory, for it has never been verbal! The silence of language, nostalgic for the silence of childhood, no longer even refers to what was felt in childhood. It is only the shadow of language, at the foot of language, contiguous to language. And if it really were a matter of restoring experiences that were undergone long before the apprenticeship of the spoken word, one would have to appeal instead to the power to speak the whole, not to the powerlessness wherein a pseudo-"silence" might nobly lock itself up, yet like an actor, like a hypocrite, like a smooth talker, like an impossible ascetic. Regression to the aphonia of the primary world is a chimera. A chimera: because this combination of properties borrowed from different animal forms is still the fruit of various stories that have been carved up and then added together. Now this is what I wanted to tell you: those actors, those hypocrites, those smooth talkers, even those ascetics deep within you are silent because they are *afraid* of the heart that was probed by those initial experiences. They do not want to reopen the wounds. Ask yourself someday: Who was Tantalus? The real may well pass before his mouth, he sees without eating; he smells without tasting; he speaks without receiving; he no longer knows how to experience the real; he no longer knows how to incorporate, gulp down, chew, absorb, assimilate the real; inside his canines, his incisors, his chops, he has nothing left but abstract words that no longer know how to designate anything about the world. He barely sees the cluster of golden white grapes and the plush skin wrapping the peaches receding in space. His two fat lips barely reach the water that eludes them as soon as they part and stretch out. Everything dries up and shimmers hazily and vanishes before Jupiter's son. It is *rhetoric* that fails him then and not the shelling-up in the uterine pouch of his mother, the Phrygian nymph, who ceased to be a possible recourse. Even, who ceased to be a hope. One can tell a depressive crisis is coming on with this sort of gap being established between the body and the real. Between the painful trismus that constrains the sufferer's jaws and the formless grub whose odor has withdrawn and whose appeal is as suspended. Between the sex so destitute and unpredictable and discontinuous and flaccid, and the wholly orificial, the shocking, the even undesirable nudity of the other, as fascinating as it is, having remained completely in dreams which the soul does not master. Between the sleep so deep and full of those images that insist on being genuine, potent, sincere, and the light become pale and dreary of an anguished, unhappy awakening, a swamp has opened, a shifting sand full of dead language stretches out—and not an auroral silence. The sensations we derive from the functioning of our organs suddenly appear difficult to us and almost unusable. The sight of our hand, the sight of the world, the sight of the blue sky in the air and the breaths that carry it and the winds that pass through it, and right up to the existence of the air, to our belabored breathing, to our struggle to breathe, to our awful, anxious choking, to our perpetually clamped neck, to our panicked fear of being, we no longer understand what was self-evident. Not the body, not hunger, not sexual difference, not verbal substitution, not the sense that oriented our movements and triggered actions, not the society that gathered loved ones together, not religion, not nature, not the universe. A confidence has been shattered. That drive, that simple little *going* necessary to life, all the little reflex muscles have suddenly retracted inside the limbs, the muscles, the arms, the feet, the fingers. Even the eyelids, for opening the eyes. Everything dislocates and one falls back into one's chair. One goes back to bed. One pulls up the sheet and hides in it the face one lost before the world. One weeps. One weeps like a man who is dying. One weeps before this flesh become meat and nearly this chaos that rejoins the inorganic.

And if one tries to recover and render intelligible what has happened, one does not succeed. If one strives to wrench from the mud the source of this awful bewitchment, if one removes the sheet, if one pushes away the cover, if one approaches this face lost in the face of the mirror one assumes will reflect it, the respiring breath fogs over its own perception, and all one can see is a poor thin layer of humid haze in the golden frame. What does one actually see through the tears that prevent sight? Like a fog from the nostrils of a deer cornered by hounds, and the beast loses himself in a cloud where his own pack devours him. The anxiety attack is an effervescence so violent it no longer permits the senses to clearly perceive what ordinarily falls within their grasp and which inverts and overturns everything before collapsing into an extreme powerlessness and a death anticipated and as though premature. It is then that language must be cleansed, not omitted. The way sight is cleansed by the dream. The way the sex straightens and rears at the whim of the involuntary images our personal demon conjures and rekindles and rouses by chance over the course of each night. The way the body is emptied and hollowed out again by hunger at the end of each slumber. The soul must be cleaned by the ancient natal vital distress. *It is its cry that the soul must restore, not its silence.* It is a sort of *fast* that it needs, that is, the opposite of exclusion or denial or taciturnity or modesty or forgetting. It needs the reminder of its hunger. It needs to *haunt*. Only the language written with great care has the power to *move* further than the death that, for the moment, *nails to the spot* this stupefied body and language become meaningless. Why hasten this death that is in any event so near and so inevitable? Why arrive so quickly at the hypothesis of an ineffable or sublime silence, when a totally other silence, a second silence, an augmented silence of language put to silence, the *silence of writing* comes to meet the silence of childhood and even partially recovers the absence of sonorous source that preceded infancy? Even more: writing *precipitates the arrest of the voice* that will so surely come in death. Writing precipitates: far from hastening this suspension, it incarnates it. It provides it with emotion and flesh. It *objectifies* it. Nature, Seneca says, has endowed us with the possibility of leaving it. We have only to raise our hand and squeeze our throat with our fingers. Death is always there like the nearest good. It is enough for it to remain the nearest. It is even excellent that the abyss, this chasm that language opens in nature, simply becomes more profound, more vertiginous. We must live on this volcano's edge that shakes unpredictably and trembles. Writing then stands before infancy the way the farewell, at the moment of death, stands before life. You evoke Titus Livius wandering through the city in flames, seeking to bid an impossible farewell to the ground of the world that crackles, bursts into flames, cracks open, and finally buries him. The word *infantia* which one finds in the ancient Romans is not a mute silence. It is all the cries and bays of nature. What the residents of Latium called "infancy" referred for them to the sensoriality that is still animal, savage, non-speaking, natural, in the living state. It is the look-out of all the senses that have just been inaugurated. It is the alert proper to bestial life that every human must continue and pursue. Rhetoric (in the use of language) is not a rampart. Suicide (in the course of life) is not a barrier. Literature is neither a thick wall, nor a citadel, nor a dam: oral language suicided and silenced in the letter is a *door* that opens very far beyond the group. It is at once an exploration, a novel space, a tidal flat, a shore. Each of us hunts all of life on the lips of our mother. But not in her *womb*, not since we left her womb. Do not go back there, for you would never make it. Do not dream of re-turning to that obscure world where you would suffocate even more. Do not think about slipping your big body into a vulva that has expelled you with all its might so you would scream with all your might to open to the light and be irradiated by it forever. Remember that words only abandon those who have hollowed them out and somewhat devitalized them. And if words resist those who are in the middle of speaking: *never* do they resist those who write. Those who write have nothing but time for them, nothing but time to go back over their sentence, nothing but time to crack open their lexi-cons, their atlases, their chronologies, their dictionaries, nothing but time to seek the help of their old, quite incomplete grammar manual which dates to the end of childhood, nothing but time to revisit, to revive, to re-etymologize, to revise, to correct, to surprise. Do not resort to stupor. Do not seek the dreadful immobility of stones and granites. I know that the fear of the soul being a phantasm is well founded. Yes, the soul, the idea of self, is only a phantasm, just as the word I is only a "grammatical person" at the heart of a dialogue it engages in with You, who is only another I, where the group's bodies fight among each other by exchanging these "grammatical persons" who are, yes, they too, in fact, mirages, and who they take to be themselves as if they were real substances. But, inside literature, it is this very struggle that comes undone; it is this dialogue that decomposes; it is the orality and sense that provoked the moaning or the racket which are ruined, dislocated, crumbled, dissipated. That is why torpor does not throw us upstream of languages, and heroic mutism does not reopen the door to the Garden of Paradise. Mutism is not uterine aphonia; mutism is not atmospheric childhood; it is only a rusty tongue or a serviceless one; a half-filled watering can forgotten in the shadow of the walnut tree; its water has darkened; a harrow neglected in a field; its singular form shines in the twilight like a preposterous branch stripped of its leaves; the little wall that encloses the cemetery blushes in the coming night; it is filled with memories that struggle to murmur, to sob. Lend your ear to this dog sighing in the warm light. Listen to this door that creaks so peculiarly! Listen to what a strange lamentation it lets out! It is such a modest farmhouse, with *hinges* spoiled by showers and time, a *watering can* eaten by rust and full of dead water, a zinc *gutter*, a *walnut tree* whose *husk*-covered fruits dangle, these are first of all words, even if these words concern things you loved long ago. Well, what are words themselves? Words are *all the things whose name you asked for long ago* when nothing designated them in your gaze if nothing came to name them. At a time when you yourself were without first or last name. That is, when you were not even the phantom your despair makes you believe you have become. Subjectivity is only a *melancholy*, a naked area that never appears so terribly as when the flow of sap and blood recedes, and not when language deserts. So work on all these powerlessnesses to speak; force, squeeze, cultivate all the distresses that course through them. The language at your disposal has the capacity of your emotion because it is the bed of it. You need not work on language to enjoy it, or to delude yourself, or to adorn it, or to respect its rules, or to seduce other people, not even to hail a woman who was lost at the moment of your birth and whose loss has pursued you intangibly since she abandoned you into the day. You need not pick apart the soul in a spirit of autopsy when it is simply a breath borrowed from the air that birth sets free. You must adore, in the acquired language, the failure of acquisition, which ceaselessly limits everything and yet never restricts language. You must fight *with* this failure to speak the lost world. Language is the *with* of our soul. It is a door always. And always it is a door that opens to whoever pushes it. Door that unhinges, window that opens, ecstasy that embarks, that voyages. The soul flies like a bird. The soul is an inside in an outside like a fish in the water that flows and invents its ungraspable form. "It is not for a fish that I weep," says Domitius, whom you quote in your letter, "but for the silence of his world and for the total absence of any gaze he might imagine on him as he moves in the element that is more his own than he himself is." You have known this world. And Domitius adds, "Sometimes a man has to weep when faced with the suffering he feels before the disappearance of what he loves. One has a right to weep over the death of animals. And even over the broad petals that fall unexpectedly from the top of a flower's stem onto the marble table where a bouquet was left and which suddenly wake you when you were so far off in your dream." You have known this world long ago and I have known this world. We have all known this existence where personal identity did not exist and the milieu was the only subject. Look at the birds hovering over the mountaintops in the canopy of the sky.

Lord, language, not being the original element of the soul, cannot be mixed with the water of the first world.

It is only a medium, a mediation, a third, a fabric, a *textum*, an artifice, the two leaves of a door, the small boat and the long fishing pole, the feather, the wing, the transport.

Hence the never-ending *work*, since it was acquired over the course of a *work* that lasted six or seven years, and it is never completely mastered by the one who suffocated in it at the end of the silence and the shadow and the water and the solitude and the natal distress. From this distress you will never be exempt. Never will a man who has learned to speak be left intact by its grip, for he has subordinated himself to it with all his soul.

Never will you be silent.

In the darkest, most obscure, most empty melancholy, if you want to survive, having left this water, you must turn this dead water into a water fast flowing and alive.

It is this e-motion you must make moving, tumultuous, rich with life, splashing.

We were screaming when we heaved ourselves from our mother's water. We commence by screaming as we suddenly suffocate ourselves at the outlet of her huge lips, freeing ourselves from the animal bush that partially concealed them. We were screaming as we slid across her naked thighs, soaked and pale. We speak a long time afterward—a little bit, very little, and only little by little—as we more or less master these great original breaths, by cutting out these specific cries, by gradually distancing ourselves from that savage, fragrant, nourishing and jealous universe.

The fact remains that we suffocate.

You, you have sunk into the sand. Philipp Lord Chandos, you stuck with Epicurus, you stuck with Menedemus, you stayed in fear, on the shore of the island of the Phaeacians, in the dryness of the wind, in the deserted granites and stones, in the powder of endless sand. You have plunged your face into that sand. But even the ships, the caravels, the tialques of Flanders, the sea barges, when they get caught in storms, can be saved by the very water that whips them up and thanks to the very wind that threatens them. That is how language is saved by the abyss. That is art. And the silence of a language is *not even* this abyss. The silence you deem ineffable is only the *opposite* of its sonorous substance. Philipp Lord Chandos, I suddenly want to give you a lesson. I want to evoke Panaetius, the incredible Stoic from Athens, who was still called Panetios when he walked along the Long Walls, unsure if it was right to leave his hometown. Once he had taken the ship in Piraeus, once he had disembarked in the port of Ostia, once he became Roman, he brought the *study* to the Western world. He called it, in his new language, *studium*. It was he who wrote, "Beauty is *in* the abyss the way it is in nature." The most serious, least tedious, most profound and insatiable of all human games is the study. It seems to me that you are still a child caught in the spray of the group's oral language, which surrounds him and projects itself over him without him understanding it, before he has so mysteriously and actively grasped it, before he has dismembered it into the shape of sentences, before he has carved it up into the shape of words, before he has rendered it solitary and silent in the shape of letters in writing. The child's choice at the end of childhood is in truth a conflict—not one that unfolds between silence and language, but one that erupts between the real and desire. Either bend before the real, renounce satisfying his desires, his needs, his thirsts, his hungers, fear that sempiternal excitation at the core of the self. Or deny the real, pursue his designs imaginatively without the least terror, enjoy his sex in the most solitary of joys, forge ahead into his dream to the point of madness. The child, to begin with, does not choose, he *tears* himself, and there is no way it could be otherwise, and that is why one must not choose.

Lord, one must *never* choose.

You are neither silence nor language.

One must always want *everything* and remain in that torn state.

It could be said that the tear is already the ego, even if it precedes it. It could be said that the tearing grows up with the ego, time, language, the body, desire once it has become genital, that is, the totally tearing joy, become sublime sexual difference. This tear is the door before the door.

We are torn.

This tearing of the two sexes is the marvel of this world.

The origin of beauty is the origin.

Sexuality, such is the truth of life because it is the upstream of life.

Sometimes time stops in lovers' arms. That is true. And it seems to be silence. And it is true that it is better for them to be silent, but this is not silence: it is all a marvelous murmuring of animals who love each other. It is all the senses that strain alert, orchestrate together, dilate, widen, play, smell, sing. True, it seems to them then like their destinies are forgotten, but—if they are really getting lost—that is because they are opening. If their abandon is extreme, then something rises, grows, wells up, pours out, flows forth. They are even on the verge of welcoming death. But it is also true that, without warning, after a certain time has passed, what opens closes back up, the desire that spread them wide abandons them. Let us tell the truth; let us come close to the truth; desire deserts humans at the heart of a genuine silence, an authentic silence, a fearsome silence, when their joys conclude. The same way the sea draws back from the shore and restores a long stretch of sand and rocks to the celestial light. And suddenly, there is much more expanse and silence. Or at least there is the distant *backwash* of waves no longer seen. Curiously, *only the language that has been so arduously acquired can break through this splitting-in-two it creates and this substitution it conducts and this somewhat opaque screen it extends over the world.* Written language traverses in silence the detumescent silence and the distaste for living. Written language is the marvelous third hand—far more marvelous than the spear-thrower used for killing or the dart that flies from it, or the bullet that comes after it in the steel pipe of your hunting rifle, when your horses chase after the does and the bucks and the stags in your park and in your forests, when your bell-ringers bring their horns to their lips, when your beaters strike their wooden clappers, when your hound dogs bark after them, when your servants holler at them. Language once written, placed before you like an object inside its new silence, manages to feel out *more and more the night, the origin, the abyss, more than muteness and disgust or denial can.* To feel out the night, such is the invention of dreams in animal sleep, in the somnolence of humans, and even in the dozing of birds. Panaetius maintained that there is a unity upstream of the world that goes back to the night, to the heavens which made the earth, to its boiling iron core, to the water snatched from the stars that avoid it, to the ancient light of black obscurity which stands, at the origin of time, threatening to explode, beyond the stars. Hesiod said that the first of the gods was Chaos half-opening. There is no meaning at the end of languages but the words, for they have the properly infinite power to tear apart the world by signifying it, preceding their own morphogenesis and repatriating to its storm. The discordant languages then add to the explosive discord that makes up the ground of the universe. They too, in turn, multiply the beings of this world which they indicate by denaturing them, by dematerializing them, by distinguishing them, by opposing them, by atomizing them. If unity bursts without end, if the torrent rushes down, everywhere the source surfaces inside the flow—and without cease, within the order of language, a more and more dissident and miraculous fragmentation occurs which nearly tunes itself to the old chaotic flow of time.

Then the tide—the mass of the ocean—returns over the deserted expanse.

Youthfulness and not *communion* with the universe.

For no man who speaks, because his throat is too choked by that subjectivity that seizes speech, that inhabits the voice like a person, that populates the soul like a crowd, can unite himself completely with this explosion since he keeps tearing it apart by speaking and by persuading himself that he alone, among all the animal, plant, or physical species, is at his own verbal source.

And yet he *touches* these *pieces*, as if he were playing with the lost sex of a God who had been dismembered. That at least is how the ancient Egyptian myth recounts it, where the only thing missing from the dismembered god is the unfindable sex which one searches for everywhere.

Fragment by fragment. Sex by sex. Tearing by tearing. Letter by letter.

The sublime cliff attacked by the ocean (and which the latter destroys as it gives it its shape), the incomprehensible depression (where the soul decomposes), the dead (the incurable and so to speak infinite distress they leave behind), the hearing of the music's lament (eternally in mourning), the writing of the spoken language (its miraculous objectivization on the page, its total silence, new and majestic), love (the passionate, intimidating, grave, restrained denudation of sexual difference), all count among these fissures through which another state henceforth impossible, *antiquissime*, appears for an instant.

Like the piece of blue sky in the lightning bolt that abruptly comes to tear apart the stormy night.

It is by way of this enigmatic necrosis that our destiny perhaps re-merges with the origin of the origin.

It is with the help of this impulsive fragmentation that our fingers take on a distinct shape, that our teeth stand up under our lips, that our eyes become round, unseal, take on color, focus, and finally contemplate.

It is by following this *élan*—this *pulsio*, this *ormè*, this *e-motio*—that the embryo becomes fetus, that the fetus grows, curls, straightens, punctures the wineskin pouch at the base of its mother, distends the lips of her vulva, tears itself from her, springs up in the world, screams, breathes.

There is a movement in the wave that advances. There is a movement in the wave that at the same time folds into itself, that retrocedes so that the wave will roll and advance. There is a prelinguistic perception inherent to depression, and it is, to be exact, like an *embryogenesis recommenced*, which is precious as a treasure. It looms in the image of the dream. It retracts itself in the spoken language. Its little images "reconfigure" in the written letters.

My friend, we bring something back from the underworld.

When the national language withdraws, the real is discovered and, behind the real, nature and, behind nature, the earth and the sky.

Then suddenly there is a sort of cry. That is *very precisely* your letter dated 1603. That is the *beauty* of your letter, Chandos, though in no way its *substance*. It is this prodigious perception stripped of semantic meaning that suddenly inhabits it. It is not its content; it is its brilliance; its bursting. It is this *nascent* sensation; and yet this nascent sensation, owing to the written language which henceforth carries it, is strictly speaking a *renascent* sensation. It is not sorrow, or an outbreak of sadness: it is an ecstasy and even a farewell. An ecstasy half-animal for its shakiness, half-human for the work it nonetheless demands—and it is even divine, Panaetius said, for the study its leisure pursues. Your letter is that very first language which draws attention to the accursed share of ordinary things and of the inconsolable sobs of newborns, to the infancy of animals, of puppies, of chicks, of ducklings, of buds, of onions, of bulbs, of seeds, to the sublime reluctance of little ones to acquire

PASCAL QUIGNARD

socialization and even obedience, to the arduous and spiky outside-language of stones, to the thrust proper to the earth, to the chaotic tide of the stars which are the true goddesses. Your language suddenly becomes poem. Contrary to your arid, dried up, confiscated soul, it has become liquid, flowing, lively once more. It begins afresh to name. Again you hail this world. Hofmannsthal, do not abandon poetry! Hofmannsthal, Chandos, both of you rightly dwell on Crassus, who fell in love with a horrible moray eel. But you forget to mention that it devoured the *living children* Crassus threw into the water of his swimming pool by whirling them over his head. And indeed, the advent of language in nature created a world that ferociously exterminated the fauna, cruelly the flora, irrevocably the water, the wind, the currents, the ice floes, the eternal snows of the world or rather of the pure "milieu" that preceded the world. And each human life recommences this discession and this painful withdrawal from a former realm, totally other, from a former era, totally unattainable. And each body, totally natural, totally *animal*, must reconquer them, must *neighbor* them, to become alive again, to become totally *animated* once more. Understand this point well: that other world is not silence. It is so much richer than silence. It is far more substantial than the void. It is much more primordial than birth itself and stands upstream of it. Silence is only the opposite of speech once acquired. *Silence is what the language we have learned invents as its opposite so that language will emerge.* You were looking for aphasic states in the sense of states prior to language. But the states prior to language are not silent states. Consider the waves! In truth, we are dealing with a sort of *tidal bore at the bottom of life.* The sea suddenly returns to the estuary. It overflows the shores the current had nonetheless, by its force, hollowed out, fragilized, delimited. We are dealing with *ecstasies of language.* After the emotional, sensorial, aquatic *aphonia* comes the chaotic, irradiating, howling *infantia*; after that atmospheric animation, the language spoken by the group is learned, taught word after word, name after name, enslaving; after the language spoken by all, written language expands, keeping to itself, silent, solitary, involuted, literary. Do not mistake the silence! What an extraordinary destiny, this incredible drive within us. We must come from the world of acquired language by seeking to rejoin the first world so we can begin to contemplate the earth in the aging of the days that go by. Here the Stoics are right against the disciples of Epicurus. To contemplate, after having lived and after being born, is to come alive again in the wake of a rebirth. It is to be dazzled after having seen. Study comes from the sky itself and proceeds directly from the sun.

4

THERE IS A KEY THAT NEVER DRIES

———

La Rochefoucauld wrote, at the end of the *Portrait* he did of himself, in 1658: Although I have a good enough command of my language, and my memory is fortunate enough, and I do not think things confusedly, I give such great attention to my *sorrow* that I often express quite poorly what I mean.

There is something, in the depths of the psyche, he says, even at the heart of happiness, which *grieves*.

The curious name for the soul, according to La Rochefoucauld, is this word, so beautiful: *chagrin*, grief.

It is an old word that comes from the dukedom of Burgundy, that referred to a rough skin used to polish, to file, and that became a sorrow that gnaws.

A dreg that settles at the bottom of experience.

A kernel of the unsaid that clutches the heart.

A disappointment or an affliction that cannot be expressed in the language of all and that poisons.

Something that is said so poorly, and the saying of it brings no joy.

There is a key that never dries. It is the key that would unlock the origin. The key to the forbidden room. The key that would crack open the space where the scene whose fruit is our body took place. One does not know if it is stained with semen or with blood. One hesitates always. Strange glue that sticks perpetually. La Rochefoucauld did not like friendship. It is bland once one has known love, he said. Everything must rise from the ancient world as if drenched in sexual viscosity. Only love impassions the bonds between woman and man. All of a sudden a crazy trust and an insatiable fear cleave to each other, attract each other, embrace each other, love each other.

Something *sticks* to the skin in the feeling so violent of love, something that is no doubt another body, which no one sees on you but you.

His twin brother, François Perrault, had died in 1628. La Rochefoucauld was living on Rue des Petits Champs at the time. Charles Perrault (the surviving twin) published his *Tales of Times Past* on Rue Saint Jacques, in 1697.

It so happened, long ago, that all the women fled from a man who had a long beard that was all blue.

What disgusted them even more was that he had already married several of them who had disappeared.

"I must go away, my love. Here are the keys. Here is the key to the gold dishes. This one is for the safe. These are for the jewelry boxes that contain the gems. As for this key, take care of it, it is the key to the closet at the end of the gallery that is below. Be careful not to use it. I strictly forbid you to enter that little closet that is located at the bottom of our house."

The immense and swaying and noisy mass of the sea, where life originated, which advances along the shores, which cuts them into gullies, which fragments and submerges them, as far as the eye can see, is all blue.

The atmospheric layer, like a thin scarf that protects us from the emptiness of the sky, is marvelously blue.

The word coalescence in Latin names everything that binds. Love also "crystallizes" the elements of the soul, just as desire "coagulates" its seeds in the body. *Coalescentia* defines the operation whereby blood clots and blackens when it is exposed to the free air.

The limestone, so pale, that holds the stones in the wall together.

The rennet that thickens the milk's surface and little by little swells its volume in the tinplate can.

Little mistletoe ball between white and gray like a pearl, though it is smaller than a pearl, little drop of light that falls from the branch of the oak swaying between the ground, the moss, the clouds—which sticks in winter if you reach your fingers out to grab it.

One can neither foresee nor hope for what happens once the body entrusts itself to nature. It is sublime. It is even unhoped for.

＊

PASCAL QUIGNARD

Upon the spring awakening at age twelve, or age thirteen, or age fourteen, the young lady, the young man feel somewhat embarrassed before this water of the other world which impregnates the fingers for the first time, or which all of a sudden settles on the lips. This original glue goes back to Eden. This tear comes to coincide then with the sadness that is born when curiosity subsides and desire diminishes. Even, this humble disgust it provokes keeps pleading for the mystery that came before it. This care that was initiated before the upheaval of nudity is indistinguishable from the compassion brought about little by little by the amazement of denudation. For there is a charity that love demands, which perhaps requires age, and that must be returned to indecency. It is necessary to have felt the delicious spread of intimacy, the scent of natural skin, its suint, like a moist halo, like a fragrant nimbus unique to each, like no one else's, that secret trust in the body's openings and their impulsive muscles, the abandon of shared sleep and almost its muffled panting, the lucidity and tenderness that begins in deexcitation and continues in languor, the immediate fatigue, *sine medio*, without a third, savage, the disheartenment itself, the *taedium vitae* which is like a secret accord of birth and death.

There is not a single scar, on skin grown old, that does not suppurate.

There is nothing that dies completely.

Not a single wound that does not, over time, reinjure itself, and worsen.

Not a single pain that does not, suddenly, rejoin the first terrible cry.

They bring their hands closer. They clasp them together. They wrap their flesh with their arms. They kiss each other. They enlace. They agglutinate. They melt into each other. The ancient Romans employed the verb *coalescere*.

When copper and sand effervesce under the violence of the flame, they fuse together. *Coalescere.*

Often words are welded together, they become one. Coalescents.

The embryo that takes shape in the water, coagulating, hanging on.

The face that freezes in the air, that stops moving.

The breath that is held in, as when one dives.

The eyes that roll back suddenly, the white that appears, the white that is the bottom of the soul.

A connivance, all the shame of it swallowed down, opens into enchantment.

Suddenly the cry that was not learned surfaces on the moist, half-opened lips.

How very far from silence, this cry so much older than every language!

This hoarse and reedy groan, this discreet belling that nearby pleasure tears from the mouth, that it manages to let loose from the back of the tightening throat, though they both hold back a little bit of the breath of life to offer it to the ascent of joy.

The soul, unwilling though it may be and without choosing to, abandons itself to the poor song where all the songs are engendered.

What a strange tear love sheds!

What utter destitution of the phlegm whose cause is unknown, whose spurt takes us by surprise, that impregnates, that attaches.

The modesty and vulnerability of this moment belong to marvel. Its contingency is perhaps the hardest part of the experience of passion. For that is what demands the greatest courage: to accept ecstasy.

How bold these eyes that close, spontaneously in sleep, irresistibly in death!

*

She wandered all through the house. She opened everything. She unsealed everything. She discovered everything. She unlocked everything. Then she became curious about what had been so strictly forbidden to her. She went down.

She went down.

She went down by a small hidden staircase with such haste that she thought she might break her neck. She took the little key and tremblingly opened the door. At first she saw nothing, it was so dark. Then she began to see the floor covered in blood and, mirrored in the blood, the bodies of several dead women, and she thought she too was going to die, and the key dropped from her hand. She picked it up. She locked the door. She went back up to her room. Having noticed that the key to the closet was stained in blood, she wiped it two or three times, but the blood did not come off. She washed it with a white bar of soap, she scoured it with sand the way one scours the coppers, she scraped it with the sandstone pumice used for digging out the stove and for restoring and smoothing down its iron, but no matter, the blood stayed on it forever, for the key was fey and there was no way to ever get it clean. If the blood was removed from one side, it came back on the other.

"Why is there blood on this key?"

"But I have no idea!" exclaimed the young woman who had suddenly become paler than death.

"You must die at once!"

With one hand he pulls her by the hair, with the other he grabs the knife. He pulls her hair even harder.

"Commend yourself to God," he murmurs as he raises his arm.

Stéphanie Boulard is a Professor of French and Film and Visual Arts Studies at Georgia Tech. Her research centers on the relationship between word and image, and the aesthetic and political dimensions of literary and artistic thinking. Her publications include *Ego Hugo* (2011), *Rouge Hugo* (2014); two special issues of *SITES* (2014) and *Tangence* (2017) on Pascal Quignard; *Ententes—à partir d'Hélène Cixous* (2018); and *Hugographies: Rêveries de Victor Hugo sur les lettres de l'alphabet* (2022). Her current research interrogates writers' collaborations with artists, exploring different links and perspectives between the readable and the visible, and her new book project is on literature, visual arts and ecology.

Timothy Lavenz is a poet, philosopher, and translator specializing in the philosophy of poetry and post-religious mysticism and messianity. In 2023, he released his inaugural poetry collection, *The Altar-Gray Gaze of a Showman on the Brink*. His writings have been featured in *Epoché Magazine*, *Oraxiom Journal*, *Kunst und Kirche*, and *Sequestrum*. His present work is focused on the hiatus of speech between language and the human real, in relation to voice, idiom, perception, and the self-emptying of being.

Jean-Luc Nancy (1940–2021) was a French philosopher. His long career saw a wide range of books on various thinkers, art, film, and the ideas of community, justice, and freedom. Nearly all his major works have been translated into English, including *The Inoperative Community*, *The Birth to Presence*, *The Experience of Freedom*, *The Gravity of Thought*, and *Being Singular Plural*.